P9-CBI-328

DISCARD

EWE

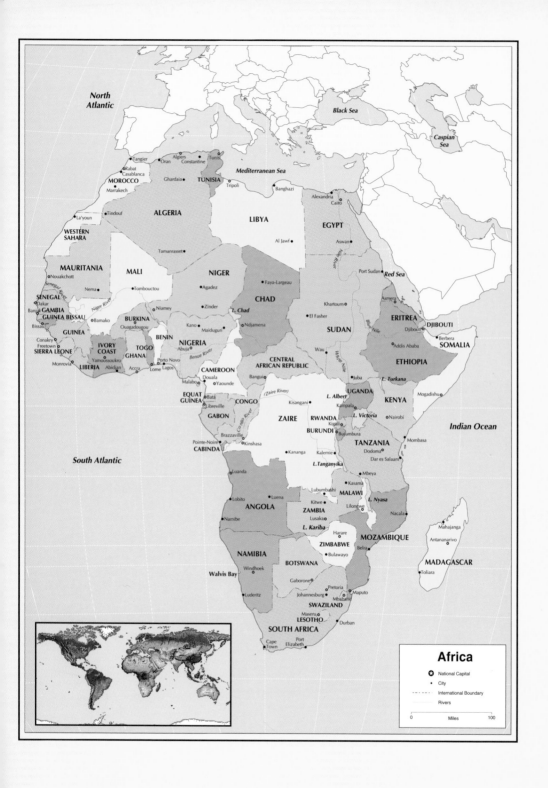

North
Atlantic

Black Sea

Caspian
Sea

Tangier
Rabat
Casablanca
MOROCCO
Marrakech
Algiers Tunis
Oran Constantine
TUNISIA
Ghardaia
Tripoli
Banghazi

Mediterranean Sea

Alexandria
Cairo

EGYPT

ALGERIA

LIBYA

La'youn
Tindouf
WESTERN
SAHARA

Aswan

Tamanrasset

Al Jawf

Port Sudan *Red Sea*

MAURITANIA
Nouakchott
Nema

MALI

NIGER
Agadez

Faya-Largeau

CHAD

Asmera
ERITREA

DJIBOUTI

Tombouctou

Zinder

Khartoum

Djibouti

SENEGAL
Dakar
GAMBIA
Banjul
GUINEA BISSAU
Bissau
GUINEA
Conakry
Freetown
SIERRA LEONE
Monrovia
LIBERIA

Niger River
Niamey
Bamako
BURKINA
Ouagadougou
Kano
Maiduguri
Ndjamena

L. Chad

El Fasher

Wau

SUDAN

Berbera
Addis Ababa SOMALIA
ETHIOPIA
L. Turkana

Blue Nile
White Nile

BENIN
NIGERIA
Abuja
IVORY
COAST
Yamoussoukro
GHANA
TOGO
Abidjan
Accra
Lome
Porto Novo
Lagos
Benue River

CAMEROON
Douala
Malabo
Yaounde
Banqui

CENTRAL
AFRICAN REPUBLIC

Mogadishu

Juba

L. Albert

UGANDA

KENYA

EQUAT
GUINEA
Bata
CONGO
Brazzaville
GABON
Libreville

(Zaire River)

Kisangani

Kampala
L. Victoria
Nairobi

ZAIRE

RWANDA
Kigali
BURUNDI
Bujumbura

Congo River

Pointe-Noire
Kinshasa
CABINDA

Kananga

Indian Ocean

South Atlantic

TANZANIA
Dodoma
Dar es Salaam

Mombasa

Kalemie

L.Tanganyika

Mbeya

Luanda

Kasama

Lobito
Luena
ANGOLA
Namibe

Lubumbashi
Kitwe
ZAMBIA
Lusaka

MALAWI
Lilongwe
L. Nyasa

Nacala

L. Kariba
Harare
ZIMBABWE
Bulawayo
MOZAMBIQUE
Beira

Mahajanga
Antananarivo

NAMIBIA

BOTSWANA

Windhoek

Walvis Bay

Gaborone

Luderitz

Johannesburg

Pretoria
Maputo
Mbabane
SWAZILAND
Maseru
LESOTHO
Durban

MADAGASCAR
Toliara

SOUTH AFRICA

Cape
Town
Port
Elizabeth

The Heritage Library of African Peoples

EWE

E. Ofori Akyea

THE ROSEN PUBLISHING GROUP, INC.
NEW YORK

Published in 1998 by The Rosen Publishing Group, Inc.
29 East 21st Street, New York, NY 10010

First Edition

Manufactured in the United States of America

Library of Congress Cataloging-in-Publication Data

Akyea, E. Ofori.
    Ewe / E. Ofori Akyea. — 1st ed.
        p.   cm. — (The heritage library of African peoples)
    Includes bibliographical references and index.
    Summary: Discusses the history, culture, and daily life of the Ewe
peoples living in Ghana, Togo, and the Benin Republic.
    ISBN 0-8239-1980-3
    1. Ewe (African people)—Juvenile literature. [1. Ewe (African
people)]   I. Title. II. Series.
DT582.45.E93A43   1998
966.8'004963374—dc20   96-32826
                                                                    CIP
                                                                     AC

Contents

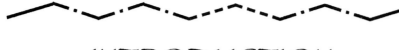

INTRODUCTION

THERE IS EVERY REASON FOR US TO KNOW something about Africa and to understand its past and the way of life of its peoples. Africa is a rich continent that has for centuries provided the world with art, culture, labor, wealth, and natural resources. It has vast mineral deposits, fossil fuels, and commercial crops.

But perhaps most important is the fact that fossil evidence indicates that human beings originated in Africa. The earliest traces of human beings and their tools are almost two million years old. Their descendants have migrated throughout the world. To be human is to be of African descent.

The experiences of the peoples who stayed in Africa are as rich and as diverse as of those who established themselves elsewhere. This series of books describes their environment, their modes of subsistence, their relationships, and their customs and beliefs. The books present the variety of languages, histories, cultures, and religions that are to be found on the African continent. They demonstrate the historical linkages between African peoples and the way contemporary Africa has been affected by European colonial rule.

Africa is large, complex, and diverse. It encompasses an area of more than 11,700,000 square miles. The United States, Europe, and India could fit easily into it. The sheer size is an indication of the continent's great variety in geography, terrain, climate, flora, fauna, peoples, languages, and cultures.

Much of contemporary Africa has been shaped by European colonial rule, industrialization, urbanization, and the demands of a world economic system. For more than seventy years, large regions of Africa were ruled by Great Britain, France, Belgium, Portugal, and Spain. African peoples from various ethnic, linguistic, and cultural backgrounds were brought together to form colonial states.

For decades Africans struggled to gain their independence. It was not until after World War II that the colonial territories became independent African states. Today, almost all of Africa is ruled by Africans. Large numbers of Africans live in modern cities. Rural Africa is also being transformed, and yet its people still engage in many of their customs and beliefs.

Contemporary circumstances and natural events have not always been kind to ordinary Africans. Today, however, new popular social movements and technological innovations pose great promise for future development.

George C. Bond, Ph.D., Director
Institute of African Studies
Columbia University, New York

The Ewe have a rich history. At public festivals, people remember and celebrate their cultural heritage. Seen here is an Ewe family at a festival in Notsie, Togo. The man holds a staff covered in gold, which is used by the spokesmen of Ewe chiefs. Both the man and woman are wearing handwoven *kete* cloths.

1

THE LAND AND THE PEOPLE

The crab says that though he may be walking sideways in a drunken manner, he has not lost his way. (Ewe proverb)

THE EWE LIVE ALONG THE ATLANTIC COAST of West Africa, between the Volta River in the west and the Mono River in the east. Today this area is part of three countries: Ghana, Togo, and Benin. It is estimated that there are between 3 and 5 million Ewe-speaking people living in these countries.

The Ewe are divided into numerous subgroups, called *dukowo* (chiefdoms). Each chiefdom (*duko*) is ruled by a paramount, or chief. Below him are many minor chiefs.

▼ LANGUAGE ▼

Ewe from different regions speak different dialects of the same language. Each dialect can be understood by all Ewe.

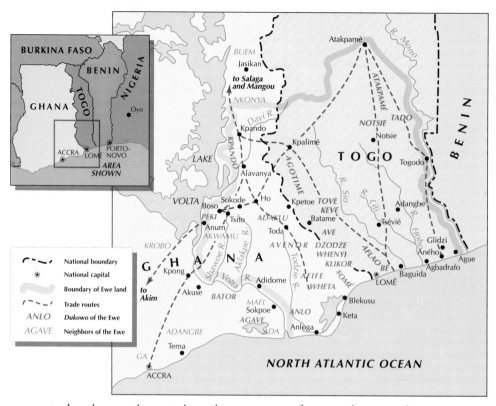

Today the Ewe live mainly in the countries of Togo, Ghana, and Benin. Some Ewe *dukowo*, or chiefdoms, are marked on the map.

In the 1800s, German missionaries combined elements of several Ewe dialects to produce a written Ewe language. This created major confusion. Experts are now working on an improved version of written Ewe.

The Ewe language belongs to a larger group of languages called Akan languages, which are spoken by several peoples, including the Asante and Fante people of Ghana. In fact, the Akan peoples share other cultural similarities besides language, for example styles of weaving and music.

The Ewe are expert fishermen. The fishermen seen here are hauling in their fishing net on the beach at Lomé in Togo.

▼ THE LAND AND ECONOMY ▼

Today Ewe territory is composed of three main geographical regions: coastal lowlands, central plains, and northern highlands.

Although the lowlands get very little rainfall, they are the most heavily populated region. Lomé, the capital of Togo, is on the coast. Ewe who live on the coast are excellent fishermen. They not only fish in their home waters but go on fishing expeditions as far west as Senegal and as far south as the Congo River.

In addition, these coastal dwellers are also expert farmers. They have learned to make the

most of the soil and climate of the lowlands.
Women do much of the farmwork and the selling of produce. They use this income to help
support their households.

A serious environmental challenge now faces
many coastal Ewe groups. The coast of West
Africa, from the Bight (Bay) of Benin to the
estuary of the Volta River, is eroding. Whole
towns and villages have been forced to move
inland to avoid being swallowed by the sea. The
coastal Ewe's means of subsistence are being
destroyed, because the fertile farmland along
the ocean is disappearing. Keta was once an
important commercial and administrative town
but the sea there has crept almost one mile
inland; as a result, Keta has virtually disap-
peared.

Ewe who live in the central plains and highlands also farm for a living. Their work helped
make Ghana the world's leading producer of
cocoa for many years.

Ewe who live in cities work in a wide
variety of occupations and contribute to the
modern economies of the countries where they
live.

One traditional occupation that survives is the
weaving of *kete*, a traditional Ewe cloth that is
similar to the *kente* cloth of the Asante. In the
past people wove at home and sold their work.
Today entrepreneurs increasingly organize

The Ewe have a long tradition of weaving. The cloth on the right includes a number of symbols that refer to leadership. The stool and curved sword (seen along the top of the cloth) and the umbrella (seen at the bottom) are all items used by Ewe chiefs. This kind of cloth, called *afevo*, is often worn on special occasions.

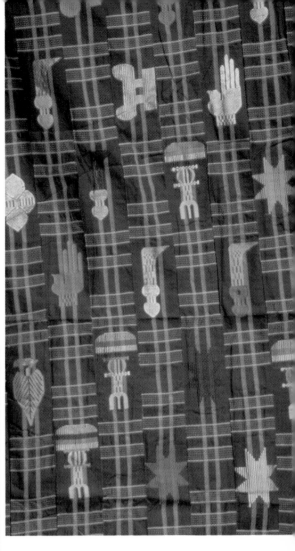

The Ewe cloth on the left is a kind of *kete* cloth called *asimevo*. *Kete* is similar to the *kente* cloth woven by the Asante people of Ghana, which has become famous all over the world. *Asimevo* cloth is less expensive and worn more often than *afevo* cloth.

Many Ewe today make a living from the weaving industry. The billboard above advertises a weaving enterprise in the town of Kpalimé, Togo. The women below work together in the market of Agbozume in Ghana selling cloth dyes.

women and young people who have left school
to weave full time for a salary.

▼ ORIGINS ▼

More research needs to be done on the early
history of the Ewe. It is thought that the Ewe
migrated from the east about 500 years ago.
They were originally part of the Oyo Kingdom
of the Yoruba people in Nigeria. During wars in
the 1300s, many of the Oyo people fled west to
Kétou in present-day Benin.

In Kétou, the Ewe separated themselves
from the other refugees and began to establish
their own identity as a group. The Ewe con-
sider Kétou their original home. They call it
Amedzofe, meaning the origin of humanity, or
Mawufe, meaning home of the all-powerful
Supreme Being.

Due to Yoruba attacks and conflict between
the various peoples in Kétou, a large section of
the population moved west again in the late
1400s. They moved in two large groups.

The first group, including both Ewe and
non-Ewe, settled at Tado in Togo after 1450.
Archaeologists in Tado have recently discovered
pottery from the 1400s that closely resembles
pottery made by Ewe women today. Some
of these migrants split away from the main
Ewe group at Tado and settled even farther
west.

SOME EWE *DUKOWO* (CHIEFDOMS)

HIGHLANDS (West)	PLAINS (Central)	COASTAL (South, East)
Agu	Abutia	Afife
Awudome	Adaklu	Agave
Hohoe	Agotime	Anlo
Kpalimé	Akovia	Ave
Kpando	Ho	Bé*
Kpedze	Bator	Bobo
Matse	Hodzo	Fenyi
Peki	Klevi	Gamé
Ve	Kpenoe	Klikor
Wodze	Sokode	Somé
	Takla	Tantigbe
		Tavia
		Togo
		Tsévié
		Tsiame
		Wheta

* The Bé later became the Agoenyive, Baguida, and Lomé groups.

The second group of migrants fled Kétou later. They stopped for only a short time in Tado before moving on to settle in Notsie, in the south central region of Togo, around 1600. In this second group were the Anlo, Bé, and Agu, together with the bulk of all the people that later came to be called the Ewe. All of these Ewe migrants who came to live in Notsie were collectively known as Dogboawo, after the name of one of the towns in which they stopped on their way to Notsie.

Like Kétou, Notsie was a walled city. The city was divided into sections, each governed by a clan chief. A king was the supreme leader. The early kings of Notsie ruled well and the kingdom flourished.

Trouble at Notsie began when King Agokoli came to the throne in about 1650. He made his people perform cruel tasks, such as kneading clay filled with cactus thorns, and waged reckless wars. Many Ewe decided to escape. The women targeted specific areas of the wall on which to throw their dirty water each day. The water soon weakened the earthen wall to the point where the people could break through and escape.

Many colorful legends about the escape have been passed down over the generations. One is that the Anlo told the people of the Bé *duko* to empty the grain storehouses and scatter grain behind the fleeing people. Pigeons came to eat the corn, and their scratchings covered the tracks of the people. Thus, to this day, the pigeon is sacred to the Bé *duko*.

▼ HOGBETSOTSO ▼

The annual Hogbetsotso celebration commemorates the escape from Notsie. It takes place on the first Saturday of November.

Preparations begin as early as August. A schedule is drawn up for the physical and ceremonial cleansing of Ewe *dukowo*. The cleaning

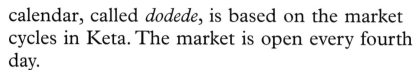

calendar, called *dodede*, is based on the market cycles in Keta. The market is open every fourth day.

If there has been illness in the community in the course of the past year, a thorough ritual cleansing takes place. After each clean-up session, special ceremonies are performed to indicate that the community has been purified.

The cleaning reaches its peak during the first week in October. At this time, people from each Ewe community gather in the main town of their region and prepare to travel to Anloga, the capital town of the Anlo chiefdom. The Anlo revived the Hogbetsotso festival in the 1940s, and Anloga is now the center to which Ewe from Ghana, Togo, and Benin make their annual pilgrimage. On the last Saturday of October, small *durbars* (gatherings of chiefs and their people) are held in the capital of each Ewe *duko*.

During the week before the final celebration, every day is filled with some activity. On Monday there is a solemn, communal meal of reconciliation known as Nugbidodo. It promotes unity and peace. The *awoamefia*, the paramount chief of the Anlo Ewe, presides over the occasion as the chief priest, although he has no real authority over other Ewe groups. Each Ewe chief publicly swears that he is being loyal both to his own community and to the *awoamefia* and is not plotting against other chiefs.

On Tuesday the *awoamefia* meets with the people to discuss projects and affairs of state. On Wednesday children entertain their elders, showing their knowledge of Ewe culture. On Thursday a general assembly is held to discuss community issues. A bonfire is made on Friday night, and the escape from Notsie is reenacted.

Saturday is the final day. It is a joyous occasion during which the *awoamefia* presides over the annual Grand Durbar. Amid drumming and dancing, he receives all his subjects, who are dressed in their finest outfits. On this day, all Ewe paramount chiefs pay homage to the *awoamefia*.

The exodus from Notsie was a key event in the destiny of the Ewe people. Once they had escaped, the Ewe split into three main groups: the northern, central, and coastal divisions. Within each of these divisions, large lineage groups, or people who share a common ancestor, split off and formed their own chiefdom, or *duko*.

Each *duko* has its own paramount chief and many minor chiefs. Each *duko* is said to reflect a division that originally existed at Notsie, before the migration of the Ewe people. However, each of the many *dukowo* has members of all of the various Ewe clans among its population, because

The Ewe chief seen here, Togbe Ameyibor X, is swearing an oath of loyalty to his people on the day of his installation in August, 1995.

people marry outside of their lineages. This creates a shared sense of Ewe identity across the political divisions between the many *dukowo*.▲

chapter

2

SOCIETY

When the snail goes on a journey he lodges with the tortoise. (Ewe proverb)

EWE COMMUNITIES SHARE THE SAME general principles of social organization but they have many local variations.

▼ CLANS AND LINEAGES ▼

The Ewe believe that every other Ewe is a relative. They believe that all Ewe are descendants of one of fifteen main male ancestors, who are thought to have been related to each other. These fifteen ancestors from the very distant past each founded an Ewe clan, or *hlõ*. Any Ewe settlement contains members of all of the fifteen main clans that make up the Ewe society.

Clans consist of a great number of members. Smaller groups of people within each clan can trace their descent to recent male or female ancestors whom they have in common. Descendants of such shared ancestors are part of the

THE ANLO EMBLEM AND SYMBOL

Each Ewe *duko* has its own symbol. The Anlo symbol consists of a cooking pot placed on a stove that has a short piece of firewood in it. This emblem is based on an Anlo saying: "*Anlo godoo lifii. Du no eme mase emenya. Naketi deka no dzome bi nu.*" This translates literally as: "Anlo deep and murky. You do not know what is going on. One piece of firewood could cook a whole meal." This conveys the idea that the Anlo are a unified and secret society. Outsiders may stay in this society without ever knowing its secrets; its people are resourceful and can make do with very little in order to create great things.

The Anlo say that the emblem and the saying symbolize their unity as a people. They look out for one another and do not allow outsiders to divide them. The symbol also suggests the way that leaders, like the stove, support their people, who are symbolized by the pot. Some believe that the Anlo emblem sums up the Ewe outlook on life more generally. Outsiders see the Ewe as keeping to themselves, sticking together, being discreet and industrious, and making do with little.

same lineage, known as the *afe* or *afedo*. Every lineage is named after its founding ancestor. Members of the same lineage are not allowed to marry each other, because they are too closely related by blood.

Lineage groups often live together in the same section of a settlement. This area is known as the *afedome,* and any lineage member is entitled to build a home and live there. The lineage owns all property. A council of lineage elders decides where lineage members may farm or which sections of rivers or lagoons they may fish. These rights cannot be transferred, even to one's children.

It is believed that when relatives of the same lineage quarrel, the bad blood between them affects the whole lineage. If one party in a dispute dies before the problem has been solved, elaborate religious ceremonies must be performed. Otherwise, a terrible disease or other disaster could strike the families of both parties involved in the dispute.

▼ HOUSEHOLDS ▼

A lineage group in any particular Ewe settlement consists of several households. As in most parts of the world, the family household, or *akpata*, is the smallest and most basic unit of social organization. The husband is the overall head of the household, but his wife or wives (the Ewe are permitted to have more than one wife) take responsibility for performing the domestic chores and raising the children.

A household consists of a compound that has several adjoining rooms. There is a sleeping room for the husband, and each wife has her own sleeping room that she shares with her children. There is also a room where visitors are

The traditional Ewe house consists of several adjoining structures, which form a compound. Often they surround a courtyard. This courtyard in Aného, Togo, is used as a religious shrine. The white stool and the containers for sacred water and herbs are used during worship.

received. No Ewe will take a visitor to see his or her bedroom.

Younger people must show respect for the older people both in their households and in society. A younger person may never contradict an older person, even in the privacy of the home.

▼ CHIEFS ▼

The Ewe adopted aspects of the Yoruba governmental system that they had lived under

In the past Ewe chiefs were military leaders. Today they are role models for their people, together with other successful members of their communities.

in Oyo. Over time, many changes occurred, and regional variations developed in the Ewe political system. Ewe chiefdoms were also influenced by their Akan neighbors. Akan influences on Ewe chiefs include wearing elaborate regalia (special dress or symbols of an office) and appearing in public accompanied by a drum orchestra.

In the past Ewe paramount chiefs were mainly military leaders. Today they have become

more like Akan rulers, who also function as the society's chief judge and high priest.

Today, of course, the Ewe live in African countries where modern governments have replaced many of the functions that chiefs once performed. The respect that was formerly reserved for chiefs is now also shown to those Ewe who have become successful and prominent through education and ability. Their achievements make them role models in their communities. Even current chiefs often admire these successful people and ask for their help. Instead of replacing chiefs as community leaders, leading Ewe today frequently support chiefs financially and in other ways. They encourage people to preserve the traditional system of chiefs and to respect chiefs in the community.

According to the traditional system of government, the paramount chief rules the chiefdom for life. However, he must regularly consult the council of elders and the council of commoners, especially when making major decisions. The symbol of the paramount chief is a stool, or *zikpui*. The appointment of a paramount chief is called his enstoolment. At their enstoolments, paramount chiefs must swear devotion to their people and to traditional rules. If they break this sacred oath, they can be destooled.

Administration is carried out by a hierarchy of officials. At the bottom of the hierarchy are

The public enstoolment of a new chief is always attended by many guests. Seen here are a group of the elders who serve the chief as advisers.

lineage heads of particular villages. They appoint a village chief. Village chiefs from various regions may hold higher offices. Higher ranks are usually organized in a military way. A senior chief heads each wing or major section of the army.

Among the Anlo Ewe, for example, the paramount chief, called the *awoamefia*, has an army commander, called the *avadada*, which means mother of war. He serves as the paramount chief's deputy and is his link with the three wing chiefs. At state gatherings, the *awoamefia* is

THE CHIEF'S BLACK STOOL

The most important object of royalty and authority for the ruling paramount chief of each *duko* is the Black Stool. This symbol has great spiritual power. The Black Stool is a shrine, and it also plays the key role in all state ceremonies. Its magical power protects the community.

After a revered chief dies, his stool is blackened by fire and kept. Stools of bad chiefs are destroyed. The black stools are kept in a closely guarded room. Once a year, the stools are all given a ceremonial bath that represents a renewal for the community.

At his enstoolment ceremony, every chief is blindfolded and led into a darkened room filled with the black stools of past chiefs. The new chief finds a seat on one of the stools. It is believed that the spiritual power in that stool surges through the new chief. Accordingly, he is then named after the past chief on whose stool he sat and whose spirit entered him. This stool becomes the new chief's Black Stool.

All stools consist of a slightly curved wooden seat supported on a base about one foot high. Each chief's stool has a different design. The stool of the *awoamefia* has four support columns. The top of his seat represents the world.

seated in the center, with his wing chiefs on either side of him. Other chiefs take their places in descending order of status away from the center, until one reaches the lineage heads.

Many of the titles in Ewe society, including that of the paramount chief of the 130 or so *dukowo*, are restricted to particular clans. The Anlo paramountcy, for example, alternates between two clans. Each of the three wing chiefs are also chosen from particular clans. A committee of "kingmakers," called the *fiafofowo*, selects the paramount chief from two or three eligible candidates of the appropriate clan. The *fiafofowo* is made up of lineage heads who do not belong to the clans from which candidates are selected.

▼ QUEEN MOTHERS ▼

The women in Ewe society are represented by the *mama*, or queen mother. The kingmakers elect her upon the death of the previous queen mother and name her after a highly respected female ancestor. The queen mother is usually the most senior woman of the clan from which the next chief will be selected after the death of the current ruler. Today factors such as education and national influence may override the seniority requirement.

The queen mother leads and organizes the women in such civic activities as running the market and keeping it clean. These are important tasks, because the market is a vital social center for the community. Apart from being a place where goods are exchanged, the market is also a common meeting place. Marriage partners often meet for the first time at the market.

In times of crisis, the queen mother leads the women in keeping the society going. When Ewe men go to war, as they have often done in the past, or when they pay visits to the royal court

Queen mothers play a leading role in Ewe society. Seen here are the queen mother's attendants during a public ceremony.

of the *duko*, as they continue to do today, the queen mother organizes the women to take over the administration. Every morning and evening she leads the women in a religious ceremony, called *bebrebe*, to ensure the safe return of the men.▲

chapter

3

RELIGION

Human beings are involved in seasoning the food already prepared by Mawu, the Supreme Being. (Ewe proverb)

THE EWE BELIEVE THAT MAWU, THE Supreme Being, created the world and everything in it. According to Ewe beliefs, Mawu used to live near people. He lived in the sky, which was so low that people could easily go back and forth between the sky and the earth. Mawu controlled life on earth. People came to his court with all sorts of problems for him to judge. After a while, however, the people became too difficult for Mawu to control. Mawu was so upset that one day he moved far away and became invisible.

▼ COMMUNICATING WITH MAWU ▼
Despite Mawu's departure, the Ewe found ways to communicate with him. Mawu left behind some powerful aides on earth, with whom he is in constant contact. These earthbound

AN EWE PRAYER TO MAWU

Oh Mawu our Father,
The source of all our being,
Give us plenty.
Let the fishermen make large catches.
Let our forests give us food.
Give us many children.
Let us prosper.
Give us victory over our enemies
And continued peace.

deities are called *trowo* (singular: *tro*). *Trowo* have the power to impose punishment in the form of drought and disease. An individual or a group can ask the deities to punish an offender or to send their requests to Mawu. The *trowo* live on mountains and in caves, rivers, and big trees. Many Ewe set up shrines at these dwelling sites. Alternatively, a special shrine for a deity, such as Sakpata, the deity of smallpox, can be built else-where for the purpose of worship.

Another way that the Ewe worship and con-tact Mawu is through ancestor worship, the key element of Ewe religious life. The Ewe have a proverb that says that when a person dies, he or she lives on as a *gbogbo*, or spirit. It is believed that if the living remember their departed rela-tives by performing certain ceremonies at certain times, their ancestors in turn will always look out for them. The ancestors influence daily affairs and interact with Mawu on behalf of their living relatives.

Mawu is therefore the ultimate protector of the Ewe, but Mawu can only be reached through deities and ancestors. Mawu's protection does not extend beyond the Ewe people. The Ewe say, "*Du bubu menyia du bubu fe ko o*," which means the customs of one group of people are not meant to be observed by another. Neither does Mawu give any protection or assistance to sorcerers and evildoers.

In front of every Anlo house is a shrine called *afe legba*. This shrine is a focus of religious worship of the ancestors of the lineage. It is believed to have the magical power to protect the household. Another shrine, called *du legba*, protects the entire settlement.

Most Ewe have an especially close relationship with a deity that protects that person from sorcery, witchcraft, and evil spirits. In some cases today, people may regard the Christian God as the one with whom they have a strong, personal relationship. People frequently carry some symbol of their personal deity with them and pray to it every day.

If someone is troubled with continual bad luck or persistent illness, he or she will visit a diviner for divination, or *ka afa*. The diviner will

In front of every Anlo Ewe house is a shrine called *afe legba* (above).
This is where the ancestors of the family are worshipped.

discover the spiritual source of the trouble, such
as an offended deity, and suggest remedies, such
as making a sacrifice.

Today only about 20 percent of the Ewe
people, especially the Anlo and Tongu, follow
their traditional religion. Most Ewe are
Christians, either Roman Catholics or Pres-
byterians; there are also a few Methodists and
Baptists. Many Christian churches combine
Christian and Ewe traditions and practices. The
best known is the Apostolic Revelation Society.
It was founded around 1950 by a former
Presbyterian called Mawufeame (man of Mawu)

Wovenu. Polygyny, a practice in which men may have more than one wife, is allowed in this church. Many of the ceremonies are similar to traditional Ewe ones.

▼ VODOU ▼

Vodou is a form of religious practice that is especially strong among the Fon in present-day Benin (who are an Ewe subgroup), the Bé in Togo, and the Anlo in Ghana. Vodou literally means a place to meet your deity. As the name suggests, Vodou is a religion concerned with the building of shrines. Unlike the shrines dedicated to one deity in particular, Vodou shrines can sometimes be used to reach and worship several deities.

Vodou, sometimes also called Vodun or Voodoo, was brought to the Americas by Ewe slaves during the slave trade. Today Vodou is alive and strong among people of African descent in the Caribbean and the Americas, particularly in Brazil, Haiti, and Cuba. In the Americas, Vodou has blended with other imported African religion systems and also with Christianity.

Each Ewe family lineage, especially the Anlo who live on the coast, sends one of its young girls to serve as a devotee at the local Vodou shrine. These young girls remain devotees of Vodou for the rest of their lives. Marriage does

The Vodou religion focuses on the worship of deities. One popular deity in West Africa and the Americas is called Mami Wata, a beautiful mermaid. Seen here are two devotees of Mami Wata at a religious festival at Glidji.

not change their devotee status. The devotees are easily recognized because each woman has been scarred. Three linear scars, about half an inch long, appear on each devotee's forehead, cheek, and on the left and right sides of her shoulders and chest. A devotee is also easily distinguished by the long, white wrap that she wears.

Devotees undergo rigorous training for about six months in order to learn about herbs, about Vodou traditions, and about divination. They also learn a secret language called Vodugbe, which they use to communicate among themselves. Any nondevotee that uses this language can bring a terrible, mysterious death upon him- or herself and his or her lineage.

The devotees at Vodou shrines serve many deities, such as Sakpata, the deity of smallpox, or Age, the deity of forests. Other deities, called *tovodou,* have a very high status because they protect everyone in the clan. They are said to have traveled with the early ancestors of the Ewe from Notsie. Individuals pray for solutions to their personal problems to deities called *homevodou.*

Vodou has a complex set of beliefs that requires the performance of specific rituals to keep the deities happy. Pleasing the deities ensures that the family will be protected from physical and spiritual harm. Since humans have very little control over the spiritual world

The dress of Vodou worshippers often reveals to which deity they are
devoted. The dot on this woman's forehead and her wig identify her as a
particular kind of Mami Wata devotee. The string of beads she wears
signifies links with the glorious past.

Many Vodou worshippers believe that twins have special religious importance. Seen here is a shrine dedicated to twins. The sculptures are clothed and given food and other offerings to honor them.

themselves, good relations with the deities are considered very important. Tending the Vodou shrines ensures the well-being of each lineage in particular and that of society in general.

There is an Ewe proverb that says, "He who gives a lot, receives a lot more; he who gives to others has done work that will never be destroyed." This is why families continue to send young girls to be trained as devotees at the shrines.▲

chapter

4
COLONIALISM AND ITS EFFECTS

A drunken mouse will never sleep in the cat's bed. (Ewe proverb)

THE COLONIZATION OF AFRICA BEGAN IN the 1800s, but Europeans had been in the region for hundreds of years before then. Their presence changed the lives of the people with whom they came into contact.

▼ EARLY EUROPEAN CONTACT ▼

The arrival of European ships on the west coast of Africa drew trade away from the ancient trans-Saharan trade routes that linked western Africa with the Mediterranean and the Arab world. All trade and economic activity began to focus on the coast. By the middle of the 1500s, hardly any trade was crossing the Sahara.

The Portuguese, followed by the Danes, the Dutch, the Swedes, and later the British and French, tried to dominate all trade in gold, ivory, salt, and eventually slaves. They often encouraged conflict between African peoples to weaken their alliances so that they could take control of them more easily.

Between 1 and 3 million people of Ewe origin were taken to the Americas as slaves. Making war and selling captured enemies to European traders became a principal activity of many chiefs. Some Europeans, aided by unscrupulous local people seeking profits, organized slave raids.

Europeans also introduced Christianity to the Ewe people. Portuguese Catholics came to the Ewe region from the 1400s on. Later, Danish, Dutch, German, and British Protestants arrived. Today new churches of local and North American origin continue to spring up in Ewe areas.

▼ COLONIZATION ▼

British rule was imposed on Ewe territory between 1850 and 1874. The British first occupied the area now inhabited by the Anlo and then extended their rule along the coast. The Germans attempted to take the Ewe territory from the British in 1884. To settle this dispute, the Germans and British decided to split the territory between themselves during the 1884–1885 Berlin Conference. The European powers did not consult the local people of the region.

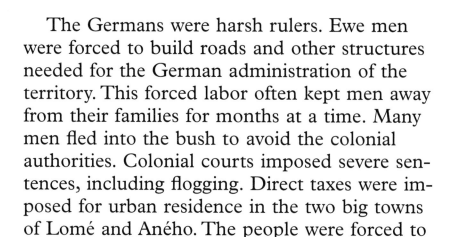

The Germans were harsh rulers. Ewe men were forced to build roads and other structures needed for the German administration of the territory. This forced labor often kept men away from their families for months at a time. Many men fled into the bush to avoid the colonial authorities. Colonial courts imposed severe sentences, including flogging. Direct taxes were imposed for urban residence in the two big towns of Lomé and Aného. The people were forced to fly the German flag. They were then taxed for flying it.

Most Ewe jobs at this time centered on farming and producing cotton and cocoa for export to Germany. The Ewe could not sell their produce directly abroad; they were forced to sell it to the German colonial authority. The powers of the chiefs were severely scaled back.

Women fared even worse than the men. While their husbands lived in work camps, the women bore the full burden of work on the farms and in the household. Women were not encouraged to go to school; instead, the Germans wanted them to produce cotton for export to Europe. The Ewe's freedom of movement was restricted. The colonial authorities frequently checked all the urban areas for people who were not working and arrested them.

These labor conditions altered the delicate balance of labor between the Ewe men and

During the colonial era, European powers divided Ewe territory among themselves. The Ewe tried unsuccessfully to unify across the colonial borders that divided them. Seen here is Kwami Fiawodzo Anatsui, the grandfather of the author's wife. He wears a woven cloth on the occasion of England's Prince of Wales' official visit to Ghana in 1925. The cloth's message—LEAN LIBERTY IS BETTER THAN FAT SLAVERY— echoes the view of many Ewe who opposed colonial rule.

women. In the past men were responsible for clearing the heavy bush for farming and for undertaking heavy labor, such as construction, while women tended the farms. Most of the men's work was neglected for many years as a result of the colonial policies.

The negative colonial experience brought the Ewe together. They formed the Ewe Unification Movement in 1912, hoping to unite their people into one country. In 1918, after Germany's defeat in World War I, Germany had to surrender its African colonies to Britain and France. French rule in Togo was no better than German rule. The Ewe in Togo hoped that the British authorities in neighboring Ghana could persuade the French to allow Ewe territory in Togo to become a part of Ghana.

However, the Ewe Unification Movement was never taken seriously by the French or the British authorities. Its leaders also failed to gain the support and involvement of the majority of the Ewe people. Instead, the Ewe's desire for unity really found expression in the Presbyterian Church. The Church had supporters in all Ewe areas, and its members made frequent visits to the three countries. They built schools and taught and preached in the Ewe language.

In the late 1950s, when African countries began to gain their independence from the colonial powers, the Ewe Unification Movement took its case for unification to the United Nations (UN) in New York. The UN organized a special vote in Togo and Ghana to measure the democratic wishes of the citizens of these countries. At stake was whether Ewe areas would remain divided between Togo and Ghana; whether some exchange of territory should occur; or whether the Ewe should form a country of their own. Unfortunately for the Unification Movement, the results of the vote were against any changes in the colonial borders.▲

5

WOMEN: THE ANCHOR OF SOCIETY

The most elegant dance by the hen never pleases the hawk. (Ewe proverb)

THE EWE SAY THAT A WOMAN IS LIKE A fountain of water. She gives generously of herself, but she can also overwhelm. Women are regarded as the anchor of Ewe society. By bearing children, they ensure that the lineage and the family are never poor. A man is the head of the family, but it is the woman who manages the affairs of the home.

▼ WOMEN IN THE EWE ECONOMY ▼

Most Ewe women are not economically dependent on their husbands. At an early age, an Ewe girl accompanies her mother to the market. There she begins to learn the basics of trading. At the time of her marriage, her husband gives her money to start her own trading business. This initial investment is supposed to generate enough income that a young Ewe woman can then run the family from her own resources.

On the eighth day after an Ewe baby is born, a special ceremony is held outdoors. Called the outdooring, this event features the baby being passed around to its female relatives. The man in the photograph holds a candle near the baby. The candle is a symbol of light and goodness; today the candle is also associated with Christianity.

She uses her profits to take care of her children. It is not unusual for women to lend money to their husbands. Among the Ewe who live away from the coast and mainly farm, it is the women who take care of the farm once the bush has been cleared.

Ewe men may marry several women, provided that they can afford to take care of the women and their children. Ewe women, however, are encouraged to be independent. This is because they must be able to fend for themselves and

47

their children. It is widely known that husbands with two or more wives can seldom provide them with regular financial support.

Ewe women along the coast are well-known and well-respected traders. They often travel long distances to trade. They go as far south as the Democratic Republic of Congo and west as Liberia. Today women often travel on planes, making trading trips both to neighboring countries and to distant places, such as Asia, North America, and Europe. Remarkably, most of these women traders have never been to school.

Economic freedom gives Ewe women political power. Women are usually present at important Ewe meetings, but seldom speak publicly. However, the men adjourn the meeting in order to consult with the women before making any final decisions. Today Ewe women occupy high positions in government, so they can often influence important decisions.

▼ THE EFFECTS OF CHRISTIAN MISSIONARIES ▼

Christian missionaries, who were a key part of the colonizing process, deeply affected Ewe family structure, particularly the position of women. They prohibited polygyny. This undermined the arrangement of the traditional Ewe household in favor of the Western-based model of the nuclear family—husband, wife, and children.

Today Ewe women play an important part in every aspect of the economy. In rural areas (top) women take care of the farm and sell extra produce at market. In urban areas (right) women are often full-time traders who set up businesses at market stalls in cities and in towns. This woman and her son sell cloth in the market in Agbozume, Ghana.

Ewe boys were educated at Christian schools to prepare them for service in the colonial administration and for work in colonial businesses. Girls were trained to become housewives. This new system failed to recognize that Ewe women were effective traders. Women did not find jobs equal to their skills in the colonial economy.

Missionaries also scorned the practice of sending young girls to Vodou shrines. As a result, the number of devotees at the shrines dropped. So too, the religious observances that were the foundation of Ewe society declined, especially in Ghana.

▼ LIFE AFTER COLONIALISM ▼
Since their independence, several African governments have tried to restore the gender balance that existed before colonialism. Ewe girls can now study the same subjects as boys in school. The result is that today women are found in all areas of professional life. Women now work as judges, government ministers, ambassadors, doctors, and businesspeople.▲

chapter

6

THE EWE TODAY

You do not apply medicine to your knee because you have a headache.
(Ewe proverb)

THOUGH THE EWE LIVE IN THREE WEST
African countries, they still have a great sense of
unity. An Ewe proverb says that a child is most
secure and safe when it is in the mother's womb,
suggesting that the closer one remains to one's
birthplace, the better. When Ewe people travel in
Ewe areas, they feel at home. They are among
relatives who understand their needs, religion,
and social customs, and who will therefore wel-
come them.

▼ STRUGGLING WITH INDEPENDENCE ▼

Ghana became independent from Great
Britain in 1957. Togo and Benin gained their
independence from France in 1960. France,
however, still maintains strong connections to its
former colonies.

The colonial experience divided the Ewe people. Those in Ghana were brought up with the

51

Ewe life today is greatly influenced by the national politics of Togo, Ghana, and Benin. However, Ewe children in these three countries still receive their early education in their own language. Parents also encourage their children to learn about Ewe traditions. This woman has brought her children to attend an Ewe festival in Notsie, Togo.

English language and British institutions, while those in Togo and present-day Benin received French education and training. It is very unlikely today that all Ewe will be unified into one political state. However, the Ewe are finding ways to keep up their cultural links while making contributions to their own countries.

The post-independence governments of Ghana, Togo, and Benin have also been building distinct identities as countries. They are each attempting to create nations out of the different peoples who live within their borders. Ewe in each of these countries have to cooperate with other nationals who carry the same passports but come from different cultures.

The situation is harder for the people who live along the borders, since the three countries are often on bad terms. The border crossings between Ghana and Togo are more often closed than open. Togo's relationship with Ghana has been damaged by the belief that Ewe leaders in the south of Togo are collaborating with Ghanaian authorities to topple the government of Togo. Similarly, the Ghanaian government is threatened by the idea that some Ewe may try to break away from Ghana. In 1960 the Ghanaian government sent troops to the Togo border to prevent this possibility.

Recently, instead of working for political changes, many Ewe have begun to turn to their

Public festivals and ceremonies, such as this event in Notsie, play a key role in continuing Ewe tradition and uniting Ewe groups from different countries.

shared culture as a way of expressing their unity across modern borders. Traditional festivals have become major events for gathering and celebrating Ewe identity.

▼ EWE DAILY LIFE TODAY ▼

In many Ewe communities, daily life still follows a traditional pattern. For Ewe living in cities in West Africa, the daily routine is similar to that experienced in urban areas throughout the world.

In a rural Ewe household, a woman's day begins around five o'clock in the morning. She washes her face and chews on a *sawii*, a stick or sponge used to clean her mouth. The Ewe properly clean their mouths before speaking to anyone in the morning. She then wakes up the older children (over seven years old). They must fetch water and help sweep and tidy the homestead. A woman is often judged by the condition of her homestead, so compounds are kept extremely neat.

The women then begin cooking and boiling water for the bath. Buckets full of water are carried to the bathroom. The women take their baths, followed by the men and then the children. Everyone bathes once a day and sometimes twice. Personal hygiene is of primary importance for every household member.

Breakfast consists of *akatsa*, a stiff porridge made from corn, and *abolo*, corn bread. The Anlo on the coast eat a lot of cassava (a root vegetable similar to a sweet potato). Their breakfast consists of *yakayake*, a steamed cassava cake. The man of the house normally eats alone or with other men in the household. The women eat with their children.

The men who fish or farm for a living leave for work before seven o'clock in the morning. Women traders leave next for the market. In the past Ewe boys generally went to work with their

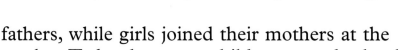

fathers, while girls joined their mothers at the market. Today, however, children attend school instead.

Ewe usually eat the same thing for lunch and the evening meal. *Fufu*, a ball made of pounded plantains, yams, or cassava, is the most common dish in rural areas. The Anlo generally eat *akple*, a sticky mixture of cassava or corn that is fermented and then boiled into a stiff porridge. These basic foods are supplemented with a wide variety of delicious relishes or sauces, made from fish, meat, or vegetables.

While the women cook the evening meal, the men gather under a tree to drink palm wine. (*Kele*, also known as *akpeteshie*, is the locally distilled gin made from palm wine.) The evening hours before dark provide spare time for experts to weave and make crafts.

After meals and washing up, the children gather around the adults. During this time, children are told folktales and taught Ewe history, values, and behavior. They also can sing songs and play games such as *oware*, a group activity that requires quick math skills. Everyone in rural villages goes to bed early. After eight o'clock at night, the streets are silent.

▼ LIFE IN THE CITIES ▼

Urban life is very different from village life. Although people may still live in compound-

THE CAT AND THE LEOPARD

A long time ago Cat lived in the forest. He and his cousin, Leopard, were best friends.

Cat was a famous hunter. He could spring from just about any position and seize his prey. Leopard, on the other hand, had no hunting skills at all. On many occasions Cat was able to catch prey that eluded Leopard.

Leopard watched closely as Cat hunted, hoping to learn some of Cat's tricks. Try as he may, Leopard could not get the hang of it. In frustration, he begged Cat to teach him how to hunt. Cat agreed, but he did not trust Leopard. He began with a lesson on how to attack prey from the front. Leopard was a very quick learner, and very soon he was adding his own tricks to Cat's techniques.

The next lesson dealt with attacking prey from the side. Even before the lesson began, Leopard, who was very hungry, tried to spring forward and kill Cat. The wary Cat, who expected such behavior from Leopard, used his agility and experience to fend off the attack. He gave Leopard a quick scratch, side stepped him, and then climbed up a tall tree. From his safe perch he addressed Leopard below.

"Cousin Leopard, since you decided to seal the well after drinking from it, this is the end of your lessons. If I had taught you all my techniques and tricks I would have been dead by now."

Fearing for his life, Cat left the forest to live with human beings. Leopard was left with scratches from the fight with Cat, which he bears to this day.

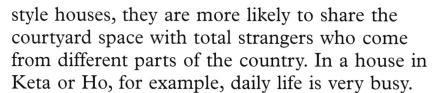

style houses, they are more likely to share the courtyard space with total strangers who come from different parts of the country. In a house in Keta or Ho, for example, daily life is very busy.

Many Ewe in the cities have intermarried with people from other ethnic groups whom they have met at school or at work. Urban populations in West Africa are very cosmopolitan today, combining people from many walks of life and many parts of the region and the world.

The Ewe in West Africa are being encouraged to see themselves more as Ghanaians, Togolese, or Beninese, rather than as Ewe. However, in Ghana, Ewe tradition is also treasured and encouraged in many ways. Children receive their first three years of schooling in the language of their region. Radio and television programming have slots for news and features in Ewe, as well as in the languages of Akan, Ga, Nzima, Dagbani, and Hausa. Similar situations occur in Togo and Benin.

The most powerful administrative bodies are the Dumegawo and the Dufiawo. The Dumegawo is the town assembly, which the mayor presides over and the *sohewo*, or commoners attend. The Dufiawo, on the other hand, is a more select assembly that consists of the *fiahawo*, the assembly of chiefs, and the *dutawo*, or civic leaders. The Dumegawo comes together to make decisions only during the most

Many urban Ewe proudly follow their traditions, as the young Ewe weaver above is doing. They add to the diversity of West African cities. Products and people from all over the world can be found in the busy urban markets (below).

important circumstances, such as serious crimes, war, and great festivals.

Today important village assemblies are often held on weekends and at funerals, since many people return to their home villages on those occasions.

The Ewe say, "It is for the sake of the future that we save the cassava peelings. They may feed the goats and sheep, or when dry they may be burned for potash to make soap." This proverb expresses the attitude that underlies Ewe pride. They know that their past resourcefulness will enable them to deal with whatever the future brings.▲

Glossary

afe (afedo) A group of people who share lineage.

afedome An area of a settlement where a lineage group lives together.

akpata The family household.

awoamefia The paramount chief of the Anlo Ewe.

cassava A plant whose starchy root is a staple of the Ewe diet.

divination The act of foretelling the future.

duko (**plural:** *dukowo*) Ewe chiefdom.

durbar A gathering of chiefs and their people.

fiafofowo A committee that selects the paramount chief.

hlõ An Ewe clan.

kete A traditional Ewe cloth.

lineage A group of people who trace their descent from a common ancestor.

paramount chief Ruler of a *duko*.

polygyny The practice of having more than one wife at the same time.

trowo (**singular:** *tro*) Deities who live on the earth.

Vodou An Ewe form of religious practice.

zikpui A stool symbolizing the power of the paramount chief.

For Further Reading

Adler, Peter and Nicholas Barnard. *African Majesty: The Textile Art of the Ashanti and Ewe.* London: Thames and Hudson Ltd., 1992.

Egblewogbe, E. Y. *Games and Songs as Education Media: A Case Study Among the Ewes of Ghana.* Accra, Ghana: Ghana Publishing Corporation, 1975.

Challenging Reading

Amenumey, D. E. K. *The Ewe in Pre-Colonial Times.* Accra, Ghana: Sedco Publishing Ltd., 1986.

Egblewogbe, E. Y. *Victims of Greed.* Accra, Ghana: Ghana Publishing Corporation, 1975.

Greene, Sandra E. *Gender, Ethnicity, and Social Change on the Upper Slave Coast—A History of the Anlo-Ewe.* Portsmouth, NH: Heinemann, 1996.

Nukunya, G. K. *Kinship and Marriage Among the Anlo Ewe.* New York: Humanities Press, 1969.

———. *Tradition and Change in Ghana: An Introduction to Sociology.* Accra, Ghana: Ghana Universities Press, 1992.

Parrinder, Edward G. *West African Religion: A Study of the Beliefs and Practices of the Akan, Ewe, Yoruba, Ibo and Kindred Peoples.* 2nd ed. London: Epworth Press, 1961.

Index

ACKNOWLEDGMENTS
The publisher wishes to thank Prof. Henry Drewel and Prof. Margaret Thompson Drewel for making available many of the photographs published in this volume.

ABOUT THE AUTHOR
A native Ewe from Peki in Ghana, E. Ofori Akyea has lived and worked among the Ewe in Ghana, Togo, and Benin. His wife, Mama Loyé III, queen mother of Woeto in Anyako, is an Anlo Ewe. Ofori Akyea has lived with his family all over the world working with the YMCA and UNICEF. Dr. Akyea's dissertation at the University of Iowa focused on the aesthetics and social role of *kete* cloth in Ewe society.

CONSULTING EDITOR AND LAYOUT
Gary N. van Wyk, Ph.D.

SERIES DESIGN
Kim Sonsky